PROPHETIC GENESIS
BY
DR. E. BERNARD JORDAN

ISBN 0-939241-08-0

Prophetic Genesis

2nd Printing

This book is dedicated to my eldest son, Joshua Nathaniel Jordan, for he shall lead with the skill and agressiveness of his namesake, Joshua, in his generation to the glory of God.

In Gratitude

We'd like to give the following individuals a special thank you for their faithfulness and support in helping to make our dream come true:

Minister Luis M. Avila

Eddie Carneal

Larry Carnes

Pastor Richard D. Eberiga

Pastor David L. Floyd

Dr. Carolyn Harrell

Ingram & Anderson Family

Camillia Johnson

Elder Fitzgerald A. King

Pastor Connie Miles

Deborah A. Thomas

Sherron Williams

Because of their generosity and obedience to the Spirit of God, we know that they have opened the door for miracles, and we believe that He shall cause the gems of wisdom that are contained within these pages to be made manifest in each of their lives, for the reward of the Lord is sure and addeth no sorrow!

In His Love and Service,

Bishop E. Bernard & Pastor Debra Jordan

TABLE OF CONTENTS

TABLE OF CONTENTS

Chapter 1
The Prophetic Flow

In the Bible, the book of Genesis is referred to as **"The Book of Beginnings"**. In it, you will discover the origins, plans and purposes for man, relationships, races, cultures, etc. It is only through the discovery of the true purpose of each, that we are able to explore the realms of boundless truth contained therein. Today, we are experiencing a time of Prophetic Genesis, where God is revealing the origins, plans and purposes for prophetic ministry as we close out this millennium.

Prophetic Principle #1

Genesis is the place of purpose.

As we analyze the genesis of prophecy, we will discover that genesis is the birth place of purpose. By examining where prophecy is birthed, we find that it is conceived in the womb of relationships, divine order, discipline, change, music, training, and pure motives.

The Church is in a critical state where we are going to go one way or the other. God is raising up individuals to function as "eyes" in the Body; He's raising up seers to give direction.

Prophetic Principle #2

The prophetic is often confused with the psychic.

In order to move in the prophetic, we must have a certain foundation and understanding of the operation of the Holy Spirit in this area. God desires for us to tap into the prophetic flow of His Spirit.

As we conduct the School of the Prophets and Prophetic conferences, we have noticed that most people have questions about the prophetic ministry. The prophetic is often confused with the psychic. We were in a particular church where a pastor, to my amazement, asked us to predict his future. We told him we didn't move in predicting the future, but we could give him the word of the Lord, or, in other words, what the mind of the Lord was concerning him.

The difference is that one is a counterfeit, motivated by the prince of the power of the air, who is satan, while the other is motivated by the Holy Spirit. Before there can be a counterfeit of anything, there has to first be the genuine, the truth, the actual, and the real. God wants the prophet to give people clarity and vision for their lives. We are not fortune tellers, but we are to give the word of the Lord.

The prophets of old did not move in prediction or foretelling, but rather, they gave the word of the Lord, revealing God's will, plan, and purpose which may or may not predict or foretell. These are the areas in which we sense that the Holy Spirit wants us to have clarity. When our thinking concerning the prophetic begins to line up with the Word, we will experience more of a prophetic flow.

Prophetic Principle #3

We ought to actually chase after God.

There are some common misinterpretations of Scripture that cause a large part of the Church to under emphasize or discredit the prophetic. In addressing some of these issues, our minds will be renewed and if we have not already discovered our prophetic genesis or birthing place, we will discover it.

*"Follow after charity, and desire spiritual gifts,
but rather that ye may prophesy."*
I Corinthians 14:1

The word "follow" means to literally "chase after"
or "to pursue". We ought to actually chase after God,
pursue Him, desire His plan, His will and His
purpose so much that whatever we do is motivated
by Him.

Paul addressed the church of Corinth and told them
to "follow after charity (love)." The Greek word
translated "love" in this instance is "agape". Love is
not an emotion, but a person. The Bible says that God
is love. Paul is literally saying "Follow after God".

We don't have to pray and ask God to give us more
love. When you say, "Give me more love," you are
actually saying, "Lord. I need more God." If you have
accepted the Lordship of Jesus Christ, then you have
God on the inside of you. At that point, you need to
begin to tap into that fruit of love on the inside of you
and it will flow out of you.

Prophetic Principle #4

There are not nine different gifts.

You are just getting started with the things of God
when you begin to move in love. Moving in love is

4

simply moving in God Himself, and is the elementary building block of your spiritual walk and growth in Him.

We are told to desire spiritual gifts. The word "gifts" in I Corinthians 12 is in italics, which means that initially, this word did not appear in the original text. It actually says, *"Follow after love and desire the things of the Spirit, or spiritual things."* As we study this, we find that it is inappropriate to separate the spiritual gifts into nine different gifts of the Spirit. There are not nine different gifts. There is just one Gift, the Holy Spirit, and He manifests Himself in nine different ways through the believer.

I believe that all manifestations are resident in the hearts and lives of the believer, and that the believer is able to move in them as the Holy Spirit sees fit and as He wills. We don't need to pray to recieve each gift individually, because we have the Holy Spirit residing on the inside of us. We just need to flow in them in obedience to the divine impulse that we receive from Him.

When the Scripture says to *"covet earnestly the best gifts"*, I believe that whatever gifts are needed to fulfill God's plan and purpose for a specific time will manifest through any believer. If a miracle, a word of knowledge, a word of wisdom or healing is needed, and you are the vessel God desires to use at that moment, the Holy Spirit will meet the need, and the virtue of Christ will be present and flow out of you.

5

Prophetic Principle #5

The Holy Spirit always does things in an orderly manner.

Gifts are given to be used to touch and bless the lives of others. As you put yourself in a position to meet the needs of others, God will bring forth the manifestations in you as He desires.

> *"For he that speaketh in an unknown tongue speaketh not unto men, but unto God: for no man understandeth him; howbeit in the spirit he speaketh mysteries."*
>
> I Corinthians 14:2

The Holy Spirit always does things in an orderly manner. The order and arrangement in the work and ministry of the Holy Spirit is amazing!

I don't believe that things happened chaotically on the day of creation. There was an order and an arrangement to everything that transpired. The Holy Spirit wants to bring order and arrangement in our lives. Paul had to deal with the church in Corinth because there was a lot of confusion concerning the operations of the Holy Spirit. The Spirit of God does not operate in confusion.

Formerly, I understood and taught that tongues and interpretation were the same as or equivalent to

6

prophecy, but upon examining the Scriptures more closely, I discovered a discrepancy between the truth and what we have traditionally been taught or may have heard and practiced.

One who speaks in an unknown tongue speaks unto God. Whenever an individual is speaking in tongues, he is speaking to and communing with God.

> Verse 2: *"For he that speaketh in an unknown tongue speaketh not unto men, but unto God".*
> Verse 15:*"...I will pray with the spirit, and I will pray with the understanding also.."*

Praying in the Spirit refers to praying in tongues. When an utterance in tongues is given, the common thesis states that a message was given in tongues. I have been in services where someone spoke in tongues and then the interpretation would come forth as a message to the congregation. I really don't believe this is possible because when a person is speaking in tongues, he is speaking unto God.

Prophetic Principle #6

Tongues is praise from people to God, whereas prophecy is the word from God to His people.

> Verse 17: *"For thou verily giveth thanks well, but the other is not edified."*

The order or administration in tongues differs from that coming from the heart of the Father unto the people to bring understanding. Tongues is praise from people to God, whereas prophecy is the word from God to His people. They are two totally different orientations and administrations.

> Verse 28: *"But if there be no interpreter, let him keep silence in the church; and let him speak to himself, and to God."*

Tongues are to be used during our private times with the Lord, unless the prayer and praise that we utter are to be used by the Holy Spirit for the edification of the body. There is no benefit to demonstrating the gifts corporately unless the rest of the body can profit from our demonstration. Tongues in and of themselves are selfish because when one speaks in tongues, he only edifies and builds himself. No one else can even say "Amen" or "so be it" to that which is not interpreted.

Sense is better than sound, and ideas are better than unintelligible utterances. If we don't know the meaning of a given sound, then we have no clarity or understanding concerning that which God wants us to do. God wants the things that we do in the local body to be understood and edifying for all in the body.

Prophetic Principle #7

Every believer should pray in the spirit daily!

Paul's instructions to the church were to let each speak in tongues, but to do it by turn so that confusion or chaos would not manifest during the services.

> Verse 27: *"If any man speak in an unknown tongue, let it be by two, or at the most by three, and that by course; and let one interpret."*

Paul sets a limit of two, or at most, three speaking, with one interpreting. Although traditionally, many have taught this scripture as a guideline to limit prophetic utterances to two or three in any given service, however, this is not what the scripture says.

Paul refers to tongues and interpretation, which is a whole different administration and order of the Holy Spirit from the ministry of the prophet or prophecy.

> *"Let the prophets speak two or three, and let the other judge.*
> *"If any thing be revealed to another that sitteth by, let the first hold his peace.*
> *For ye may all prophesy one by one, that all may learn, and all may be comforted."*
> I Corinthians 14:29-31

Here, Paul begins to set things in order. Whenever tongues are spoken, it is a display of man speaking unto God. Acts, chapter 2, states that those near the upper room on the day of Pentecost heard the newly Spirit-filled believers magnifying the Name of the Lord. There is a different order or administration for those who are moving in tongues and interpretation than there is for those who are moving in the gift of prophecy and bringing forth the Word of the Lord.

I encourage every believer to pray in the Spirit every day. I pray in the Spirit every day. Paul said that he spoke in tongues more than all of the people of Corinth. Evidently, Paul did a lot of praying in the Spirit unto the Lord.

Praying in the Spirit is very important in the life of the believer. When you don't know how to pray for a situation, you should learn how to pray in the Spirit. Often, when entering into prayer it is best to pray in the Spirit and then you will be able to pray by your understanding.

We also need to speak a language that this natural world can understand and respond to. We need to make certain confessions in the understanding so that the earth can comprehend the things we are declaring. We can't speak forth things into the earth in tongues, which is a heavenly language.

> "Moreover David and the captains of the host separated to the service of the sons of Asaph, and of Heman, and of Jeduthun, who should prophesy with harps, with psalteries, and with cymbals: and to the number of the workmen according to their service was:

10

of the sons of Asaph: Zaccur, and Joseph, and Nethaniah, and Asarelah, the sons of Asaph under the hands of Asaph, which prophesied according to the order of the king..."

...all these were the sons of Heman the king's seer in the words of God, to lift up the horn. And God gave to Heman fourteen sons and three daughters.

All these were under the hands of their father for song in the house of the Lord, with cymbals, psalteries, and harps, for the service of the house of God, according to the king's order to Asaph, Jeduthun, and Heman."

I Chronicles 25:1,2,5,6

Prophetic Principle #8

All things have ears.

This passage speaks of the ministry that was in the temple. They prophesied with the instruments. Anything that can make an expression can prophesy. All things have ears. The Bible says to speak unto the mountain and it will be removed. God told us to speak unto things. Praying in the Spirit is not enough, but you must speak a language that the earth can understand.

11

The Prophetic Flow

Although speaking in tongues is helpful in flowing in the prophetic, it is not until we are able to make a distinction between the two that we will be able to tap into the prophetic flow.

Chapter 2
Despise not Prophesying

"Despise not prophesyings" (I Thessalonians 5:20).

We should never come to a place where we despise prophecy. Though we will always hear a few "off the wall" prophecies and see errant prophets, that doesn't mean we should totally forsake the gift of prophecy in the Church.

Prophetic Principle #9

We need to prove all things.

If someone slips you a counterfeit bill, you don't react by throwing away all of your money! As the verse below indicates, we should judge prophecy to separate the good from the bad.

Verse 21: *"Prove all things; hold fast that which is good."*

We need to prove all things. Even God, in the days of creation, proved what He had done and judged it to be good. After He created man, God said it was very good. Everything that God does, He judges.

"Let the prophets speak two or three, and let the other judge.

If any thing be revealed to another that sitteth by, let the first hold his peace."

I Corinthians 14:29-30

Prophetic Principle #10

Anything that goes unjudged is dangerous.

In these verses we see the principle of witness. God will do nothing without prophetic confirmation. This also means that we are to allow others with prophetic insight to judge the value and accuracy of what has been said. Anything that goes unjudged is dangerous. Therefore, anyone who prophesies must submit their prophesy to the judgment of others. All things must be judged.

Prophetic Principle #11

As we retire at night, we should get down on our knees and judge our day.

Judgment is not a negative stance--no one is attempting to determine guilt. The power of a prophetic word is such that it can cause a person to either embrace life or death. Anything this critical, must be scrutinized.

When someone is in "critical condition", we understand that they have entered a time of reckoning; things are going to go one way or the other. Many people are at a critical place in their lives where they need to determine the outcome of certain situations before they can go on to complete their destiny.

As we retire at night, we should get down on our knees and judge our day. Become accountable to God; cultivate a moment of silence in the presence of God. Thank Him for the good and judge the bad, so it can be changed. Hold onto the good and discard the bad.

Prophetic Principle #12

Everyone has the innate ability to prophesy.

As a pastor, I frequently release the body at our local church to contribute so that all may prophesy one by one and that all may learn and be comforted. I believe that everyone has the innate ability to prophesy. We are teaching how to hear the voice of the Lord in the School of the Prophets, not how to prophesy. Once people can isolate the voice of the Lord from the thoughts of their mind, they don't have a problem speaking.

> Verse 26: *"How is it then, brethren? when ye come together, every one of you hath a psalm, hath a doctrine, hath a tongue, hath a revelation, hath an interpretation. Let all things be done unto edifying."*

God has assembled everyone into the Body with the ability to contribute something that will edify the other members. In the Old Testament, the men of Israel had to appear before the Lord three times a year. They were not to appear before the Lord empty handed. I believe that this Scripture can be looked at in the same light. The Holy Spirit has given every one of us something to contribute in the Body so that whenever we appear before the Lord as a Body, none of us should come "empty handed". We should also expect God to speak when we enter into His presence. And as He did in the Old Testament, He will speak through one of His prophets.

Prophetic Principle #13

Whenever we appear before the Lord as a Body, none of us should come "empty handed".

There was a School of the Prophets recorded in the Old Testament. Yet today, it is easy for us to identify schools for pastors, evangelists, and teachers, but scarce are the training grounds for those who are called to function in prophetic ministry.

Yet the prophets must be taught and trained just like any other ministry gift. Room must be given for development and growth into the prophetic office.

The Holy Spirit has all these things resident in the Body. We need to get in the flow by learning what He is saying and how to use the tools He has given us.

Prophetic Principle #14

The Holy Spirit is called to help us.

I Corinthians 14:31 *"For ye may all prophesy one by one, that all may learn, and all may be comforted."*

The word "Comforted" means "called to one's side". "Para Kaleo" is the Greek word translated into "comfort". "Para" means "to one's side", and "kaleo" means "to call".

The Holy Spirit is called to help us. In the Latin, the idea is expressed in two words "con fortis" which means "to strengthen by being with".

17

The Word of the Lord spoken prophetically should always strengthen us as long as we retain it. This is why we encourage people to write down the word that they receive. Then, in the stress and time of imminent fulfillment, they can pull it out later and it will strengthen their faith.

Prophetic Principle #15

Man does not live by natural provision alone, but by every prophetic word that comes from out of the mouth of God.

Before we discovered the significance of recording the prophetic word, they were unable to strengthen us because, during our time of need, they were not with us. There was a prophecy that was once given to me that blessed me greatly every time I listened to it. As I kept playing the tape, I repeatedly heard the Lord giving me a word through it about a spirit that I was up against. I would be comforted, strengthened, and encouraged whenever that prophecy sounded in my ears.

Many believers wonder why they are not as strong as they desire to be or why they don't have a stronger spiritual life. According to Jesus, man does not live by natural provision alone, but by every prophetic word that comes forth out of the mouth of God. When you allow yourself to despise prophecy, you cut off part of your spiritual life support. Therefore, you must place great value upon the prophetic words that are sown into your life.

Chapter 3
The Marriage of the Prophet and the Minstrel

One day, as I examined Psalm 149, the relationship between music and prophecy became glaringly apparent to me. I found that prophecy and music work hand in hand. The enemy does not want to see the marriage of the prophet and the minstrel, and attempts every devious strategy possible to prevent their covenantal union from coming to pass.

Prophetic Principle #16

Prophecy and music work hand in hand.

When the prophet and the minstrel enter into a marriage, the prophetic will enter a new level. As the minstrel plays, the hand of the Lord begins to move upon the prophet. It sets the flow and orchestrates the movement of what God wants to do in that service. The minstrel induces labor and the prophet gives birth to the Word of the Lord.

Prophets went without music for years. There is a real need for the ministry of the minstrel. When you look at the School of the Prophets in the Old Testament, you will see that the company of prophets were coming down out of the hills with the pipes, harps and different string instruments. You can't separate the prophets from the instruments, for they continually set the mood and the pace for the prophet.

Prophetic Principle #17

Instruments teach various aspects of timing and rhythm.

The company of prophets also had tambourines, or some type of a drum that was struck with the hand. We do not read about the drum until we read about the Israelite women playing them when they came out of Egypt. Israel got their instruments from many of the neighboring nations. The drum had its roots in Africa, and was used in their dancing, rituals and communication systems.

The prophets also used pipes, which resembled today's flutes. Their harps were the ancestors to our guitars. The string instruments, percussion, and the wind instruments were all present. I believe they had all these instruments because the Holy Spirit wanted to teach them various aspects of timing and rhythm so that they could understand how to flow with what God was saying.

One of the worst things that can happen in the midst of a service is for a person to give a word that is "off key". Have you ever heard someone sing off key? It throws off everyone's sense of direction! There are prophets who prophesy off key. When singing in the minor key, many singers have trouble maintaining their correct pitch. Staying in tune becomes a real challenge. It takes a great deal of practice and discipline to develop the skills necessary to successfully master the minor keys. Similarly, minor prophets need practice to develop their ear, for there is a tendency to prophesy off key as well.

Prophetic Principle #18

Timing is the key to understanding the mood of the Spirit.

Prophetic ministry within the local church possesses a successive flow. In other words, all the messages will be interconnected, bringing forth a series of thoughts from the Lord that will generally have one overall theme. This is why music is very important in our School of the Prophets. Music helps the prophets to remain focused on what is being declared. Eventually, all the students of the School will be involved in some form of music or art to teach them timing, harmony and teamwork.

Timing is the key to understanding the mood of the Spirit. There may be a time when a word from the Lord is dropped in your spirit, but it might not be the proper time to deliver it. When God drops the seed of the prophetic word in the womb of your spirit, sometimes He just wants it to sit there and ferment for a while. Then He will take it, serve it to the congregation and men will be able to say that He has reserved the best part for last.

In the Old Testament School of the Prophets, they understood the art, importance, and science of music, and what effects different types of music had during the course of ministry. This is how David knew exactly which music to play on his harp to expel the devil off of Saul. David spent time training in the School of the Prophets. With the knowledge that some types of music affect our spiritual warfare, and other types bring forth significant healing and deliverance, it would certainly behoove our musicians today to take note of which music brings forth which effect, so that warfare music is not played at a time of worship, and the Church can actualize the fullness of the gift of the minstrel within her midst. Music brings the anointing

Prophetic Principle #19

Music will bring forth the peace of God.

Music was cultivated in the School of the Prophets. It was placed there to soothe and quiet the soul. How many of you have ever needed your soul quieted? There are times when you have gone to church troubled and the music ushered you into the presence of God, where His reality caused all of your trials to pass into oblivion as you gave yourself over to the worship of Him. Your soul basked in calmness.

This is why it is good to play music in your homes to relieve some of the tension and the tightness that is in the air. You have strongholds in your home that provoke constant arguments. Play some anointed music in your home and let it permeate the atmosphere. Music will bring forth the peace of God in your midst.

II Kings 3:13 tells of a leader coming unto the prophet to get the Word of the Lord in a time of battle. As he approached him, the prophet was troubled. Prophets are human, too. He wanted to send him away.

The Marriage Of The Prophet And The Minstrel

"And Elisha said unto the king of Israel, What have I to do with thee? Get thee to the prophets of thy father, and to the prophets of thy mother. And the king of Israel said unto him, Nay: for the Lord hath called these three kings together, to deliver them into the hand of Moab."

I know exactly how Elisha must have felt. When you were inundated by numerous projects and campaigns where you needed assistance, this person was non-existent. Then, when he has a crisis, all of a sudden he calls you and wants a Word from the Lord! This is a natural human reaction!

Prophetic Principle #20

Music settles the conflicts of the soul.

Elisha was disturbed by this because it is not unusual for men and women to use and abuse the men and women of God. The only help Elisha could find was a minstrel.

Verse 15: "But now bring me a minstrel. And it came to pass, when the minstrel played, that the hand of the Lord came upon him."

The minstrel probably played the harp. When he played, it set the tone and the environment for the hand of the Lord to be upon the prophet. Music has a way of settling the conflicts of the soul and bringing the anointing.

Elisha called for a minstrel to soothe and quiet his soul. It is speculated that they used music to help forget the things of the earth and to begin to move in the eternal. Music has a way of elevating you into the heavenlies.

I was sharing with my music team that I love to go to Augusta, Georgia. The musicians there, though I didn't know what cords they struck, pulled me into realms that I have never been in before. There was one service where the musicians played for four continuous hours. We ventured way out into some uncharted waters. The entire congregation was way out there. We could not get back to earth!

We were prophesying in realms that we had never prophesied in before. I couldn't get over it. Nothing complicated took place, but it was just the order and the structure of the music that those ministrels played that brought forth a freedom and a liberty to yield to the moving of the Spirit in a greater prophetic degree.

I never got to my notes in that meeting! We felt the Holy Spirit ministering to the church concerning some things that were taking place in their midst. Principalities were being dealt with. We were hearing directly from God as He dealt with us and showed us some things.

All this was happening as the musicians were playing. It was totally unrehearsed! It was simply the musicians playing singularly anointed background music that set the pace for the service. We ministered for hours and could not get back into the natural realm. Eventually we had to just tell them to stop playing or we never would have sat down!

Prophetic Principle #21

There is more than one way of casting out a devil.

I believe that minstrels play with beats within the music that intertwine with your heartbeat and transform you into another man. When Saul came into the company of the musicians, they began to play and he was turned into another man.

There is more than one way of casting out a devil. David played the evil spirit off of Saul. As you, like David, begin to pull upon the strength of the minstrel's ministry, you will learn how to pull upon the strings of that person's heart and give them a change of heart.

They will come with murder in their eyes and leave with love in their hearts. The music, with the prophet, will begin to move things into a realm that is beyond the temporal.

When we have ministered in places where the music hasn't been just right, it causes the anointing to lift. The lifting doesn't mean the Holy Spirit left because it was over, but it simply means that there was an interruption in the flow. When this happens, we have the people lift their hands and praise the Lord to try to recapture the flow.

Prophetic Principle #22

The hand of the Lord is the presence of God.

Having people praise God in this situation is not a prophetic ritual, but we sense the anointing lifting and we try to bring the congregation back into a place of worship to invoke the presence of the Lord. This is why it is important to understand the relationship between prophecy and music.

The hand of the Lord is the presence of God, which enables the prophet to begin to minister to the individuals who need ministry. The minstrel causes the presence of God to manifest. In the presence of God is the fullness of joy.

A New Song

"Praise ye the Lord. Sing unto the Lord a new song, and His praise in the congregation of saints.
Let Israel rejoice in Him that made him: let the children of Zion be joyful in their King.
Let them praise His name in the dance: let them sing praises unto Him with the timbrel and harp.

For the Lord taketh pleasure in His people: He will beautify the meek with salvation.

Let the saints be joyful in glory: let them sing aloud upon their beds.

Let the high praises of God be in their mouth, and a twoedged sword in their hand;

To execute vengeance upon the heathen, and punishments upon the people;

To bind their kings with chains, and their nobles with fetters of iron;

To execute upon them the judgment written: this honour have all his saints. Praise ye the Lord."

Psalm 149:1-9

I believe that when we come forth with new songs, we shall be able to bind kings with chains. In verse one it says we must sing unto the Lord a new song and His praise in the congregation of the saints. The new song and praise are significant because, in the spirit, there are always new things to do and stir up.

Prophetic Principle #23

There is always something new in God.

A new song comes because there is to be a new deliverance. Anytime there is a call for a new song it is because there is to be a new deliverance. It represents a breakthrough, new hope springing up in the nation, and a birthing forth of new life.

The Psalmist commands us to sing a new song. We need to lock into the sensitivity that there is the newness of God. There is always something new in God.

When the children of Israel were coming out of the land of Egypt, they sang the song of Moses. Miriam used the tambourines and they began to dance and sing about how the Lord delivered them. Can you imagine the joy their liberation brought after being in bondage for so many years?

Prophetic Principle #24

 Every new day of visitation is ushered in with a new song.

They were miraculously brought out of Egypt and then watched their enemies get swallowed up in the sea. The song of Moses was sung many times as a memorial. As awesome as this great deliverance was, there came a time when this particular song was no longer suitable. There came a time for the new song about something God was currently bringing His people through.

There were the songs of Deborah and the songs of David that commemorated the move of God in their day.

The Marriage Of The Prophet And The Minstrel

There were songs of Solomon when he dedicated the temple, and when the people came out of captivity. Mary sang in response to the news that she would bear a son, Jesus. Her soul magnified God! Every new day of visitation is ushered in with a new song. It begins to speak to the defeat of the enemy.

In every move of God there is a new song. In the last five years there have been phenomenal changes in the worship songs that have been sung by the Church.

There are certain songs that are now out of place, such as *"If you want joy, you must leap for it."* This was good in the 60's during the charismatic movement when everybody was full of jubilee. We were trained for blessings, to be happy, and not for war.

Now we begin to hear a new song. We hear songs of worship, warfare and praise. I believe that every generation should experience a fresh visitation of God.

Prophetic Principle #25

Sing of your experience in God!

Many of us know what it means to weep upon our beds, but not to sing aloud upon our bed. Have you ever woke up with a song in your heart and in your mouth? Just let it come forth. The tears will be exchanged for a new song.

A new song may be an old song put in a new form. You will notice in the Scripture that God does not make all "new things," but He makes all "things new."

> II Corinthians 5:17 *"Therefore if any man be in Christ Jesus, he is a new creature: Old things are passed away; behold, all things are become new."*

Revelation talks about the song of Moses. It's like a second stanza has been added. It was also the song of the Lamb. Another dimension of life was added to it.

Psalms, Hymns, and Spiritual Songs

> Ephesians 5:19: *"Speaking to yourselves in psalms and hymns and spiritual songs, singing and making melody in your heart to the Lord;"*

Here we see singing in private worship. You need to start singing to yourself in psalms and hymns and spiritual songs. Psalms can be subject to the character of the psalmist. David often sang of his experience. You need to get a song about an experience God has highlighted in your life, and put it to music.

Prophetic Principle #26

Stay in a state of worship.

The Marriage Of The Prophet And The Minstrel

Hymns are songs of praise addressed to God, singing to Him, about Him. Like, "A Mighty Fortress is our God."

Spiritual songs are an ode, or a poem, given by the Holy Spirit. Spiritual songs are songs that are accompanied by musical instruments.

If you research the term "singing in song," it actually means to accompany with a musical instrument. Not only is it singing, but it involves playing an instrument as well.

Spiritual songs must be spontaneous playing and singing by the Spirit, from the heart in a state of worship. It is one thing to have a new song, but it is another to spontaneously bring forth a new song from your heart in a state of worship.

You should be in such a state of worship in your home and as you are walking down the street. I used to walk through the streets late at night singing spiritual songs. People would look at me like I was crazy, but I never quit. I was about 17 years old, just coming into some things of the Lord, green and still growing.

Late one night, while I was walking home engrossed in a spiritual song, I encountered a young man who asked me if I was a Moslem or something. I said "No" and kept on singing. He had walked along side of me for a ways, when the Spirit of the

Lord told me to turn and go down another block, but I said no, because my singing was witnessing to him.

As we entered into this dark area the young man pulled out a knife and demanded all of my money. I responded by singing in spiritual songs and prophesying to him. He stopped, looked at me and asked me how I knew those things about him, and who told me all those things.

Prophetic Principle #27

Singing in tongues is Scriptural.

I told him God did, that God wanted him to get saved, and he was going to church with me right then. He told me to get away from him and departed. This is why I have such an appreciation for spiritual songs!!

In I Corinthians 14:13, we can see that singing in tongues is Scriptural. When you are speaking in tongues it is not the Holy Spirit that is praying, but it is your spirit that is praying by the enabling of the Holy Spirit.

Wherefore let him that speaketh in an unknown tongue pray that he may interpret.

For if I pray in an unknown tongue, my spirit prayeth, but my understanding is unfruitful.

What is it then? I will pray with the spirit, and

The Marriage Of The Prophet And The Minstrel

I will pray with the understanding also: I will sing with the spirit, and I will sing with the understanding also.

I Corinthians 14:13-15

When you sing in the spirit and then sing with understanding that is prophetic. Music and prophecy are inseparable.

Colossians 3:16: *"Let the word of Christ dwell in you richly in all wisdom; teaching and admonishing one another in psalms and hymns and spiritual songs, singing with grace in your hearts to the Lord."*

 If the written Word of Christ is not dwelling in you richly, your spiritual song is going to be limited. Your prophetic word will be limited. Prophecy is not just seeing what is already in your life. It should be adding a dimension to your life in revelation of Jesus. Whatever is void of Jesus, needs to be thrown out.

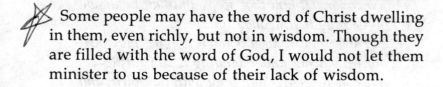

Prophetic Principle #28

Wisdom is the ability to apply the knowledge that is already inside of you.

Some people may have the word of Christ dwelling in them, even richly, but not in wisdom. Though they are filled with the word of God, I would not let them minister to us because of their lack of wisdom.

Every truth that the Holy Spirit ministers to you is not to be released right away. Not everyone is ready to receive everything; people are at different levels. Because some need to stick with the basics, there has to be a degree of wisdom in handling the word of God skillfully. Wisdom is the ability to apply the knowledge that is already inside of you.

Notice that wisdom precedes teaching and admonishing in this verse. As I meditated on this verse and inquired of the Lord, I received the revelation that the church is to begin to teach and admonish through songs. The church becomes whatever it sings.

The Lord began to impress upon me that there are some things that He wanted me to teach, but that I won't be able to teach just standing and preaching. Some of it will have to be done by psalms and hymns and spiritual songs.

God wants to begin to teach and admonish in psalms and hymns and spiritual songs because the church will become whatever it sings.

Prophetic Principle #29

Anything in music with rhythm is disciplined.

After this insight, I really began to understand that Satan seeks to separate the prophet from the minstrel because of the revelation that the prophet will receive. Once that revelation is put to music, the church will be transformed into whatever it sings.

That's why, when you begin to sing the blues, you have the blues! You become whatever you sing! The Lord said this is an area of truth that He wanted to open up. He wants to take the School of the Prophets and use music very strategically in teaching the prophets what music and prophecy have in common.

 The minstrels are musical prophets. They need to begin to take the revelation, set music to it and cause it to be sung.

The word of Christ needs to dwell within us so that we can teach through song. To teach means "to give instructions". We can see the effects of music in the way that some children respond to what they listen to. Certain rock music creates rebellion in the home, causing teens to move into sexual promiscuity, perversion, or whatever is in the song.

The passage also talks about admonishing. "Admonish" means "to put in mind". You are actually placing something in someone's mind. It also means "to warn, to train by action and to correct by discipline."

Anything in music with rhythm is disciplined. The notes and timing have to be just right in music. Admonishing will correct by disciplining.

The difference between teaching and admonishing is that teaching primarily involves expounding on the things that are wrong and calling for a warning while admonishing deals chiefly with the impartation of a positive truth. Teaching will show you the error, while admonishing instructs you in the way you should go.

When we come together there should be a new psalm, or a situation where the people are being transformed through teaching and admonishing that is in the song. This is why our songs need to be relevant and scriptural. "Swing low, sweet chariot, coming to carry me home" needs to be thrown out because there is no chariot coming down to carry us home!

Prophetic Principle #30

You become whatever you sing.

As a result, the Church is singing songs they shouldn't be singing, and are becoming what they shouldn't be. You can look at the stagnant state of the church and tell that our mentality has been shaped by "We will understand it better by and by." God is telling us to get over into the "here and now", for He is a "now" God, for "Now faith is..."

The Marriage Of The Prophet And The Minstrel

We need to understand that a lot of songs that we have sung were born out of slavery and oppression. We no longer need to sing those songs because it is a new day. We don't want to become that, so we need to stop singing them and sing the new song.

The church becomes whatever it sings. We are to sing with grace in our hearts.

 God is breathing new revelation and insight into the Church. It will have to be captured in music and articulated in prophecy. We need to know the heartbeat of God in order to tap into His life flow. This will come about as the minstrel and the prophet join in divine purpose.

The minstrel and the prophet; the two shall become one.

Chapter 4
"In House" and "Outhouse" Prophets

I Samuel 19:18 *"So David fled, and escaped, and came to Samuel to Ramah, and told him all that Saul had done to him. And he and Samuel went and dwelt in Naioth."*

When David was in trouble and Saul was after him, he fled to the School of the Prophets. The School of the Prophets is be a haven, a place of rest. When I looked up "Naioth", it was not the name of a place, but signifies "a dwelling place" or "a lodging". They went to a house of study, or a place where there was lodging for students.

In the School of Prophets, they had a dormitory--a place of lodging. Before the prophets went out and prophesied in Israel, I believe their ministry was first proven locally before they went national.

Prophetic Principle #31

The School of the Prophets is a haven, a place of rest.

There is a degree of safety, covering, protection and discipline that is developed in your life when you are connected to a local church. God uses the local church structure to raise up and stabilize those He has called to service. It is easy to recognize someone who has not first humbled himself and been exalted under good leadership. They exude the stench of an independent spirit and lack wisdom and understanding of church government. They usually present a deficit in their understanding of authority, and frequently violate and overstep their own boundaries of function through their ignorance.

Prophetic Principle #32

God uses the local church structure to raise up and stabilize those He has called to service.

I believe there are two types of prophets: the **"in house"** prophets and the **"outhouse"** prophets. Many of you know what an outhouse is. The outhouse was commonly found in the Southlands, or in extremely rural areas. The outhouse was the place utilized for a bathroom--before our present day plumbing systems were installed. The outhouse was a little shed, outside the house. There was <u>never</u> a pleasant odor there!

When you have prophets who have never been raised up in the house (the local assembly), there is an odor and a stench about their ministry and message that does not agree with the flavor and the aroma that is within the house.

Prophetic Principle #33

Whenever you come in the company of the prophets, you will prophesy.

People who are roaming from church to church have a stench; they are outhouses. They are not flowing in the vision of anyone's house. There is an odor in their ministry that is not pleasant.

There was a community where the prophets-in-training functioned.

Verse 19: *"And it was told Saul, saying, Behold, David is at Naioth in Ramah."*
He was at the dormitory or the place of study.
Verse 20: *"And Saul sent messengers to take David: and when they saw the company of the prophets prophesying, and Samuel standing as*

> *appointed over them, the Spirit of God was upon*
> *the messengers of Saul, and they also prophesied."*

Whenever you come in the company of the prophets, you will do whatever the prophets do---you will prophesy. Samuel was providing oversight. He was the senior prophet. I believe that the anointing and the spirit that was upon Samuel was transferred onto the other prophets.

> Verse 21: *"And when it was told Saul, he sent other messengers, and they prophesied likewise. And Saul sent messengers again the third time, and they prophesied also."*

There must have been a powerful anointing in that place. Three different groups of men went to get David, but they couldn't get to him. The music and the anointing of God was flowing and they entered into the presence of God.

Prophetic Principle #34

Whatever the leader has, you will have.

Paul, in I Corinthians 14, said that when you prophesy, you shall make manifest the secrets of men's hearts. I have had people in some of my services get upset at me because they thought the message was purposely aimed directly at them. I didn't give even a second thought as to whether or not they were there. The secrets of their hearts were made manifest.

Everyone doesn't love prophetic ministry. There are those who like to keep the secrets of their heart a secret. All of us have skeletons hidden that we pray the Lord won't reveal.

God will deal with skeletons in the closet and nobody will know they are there but you and God. You almost feel naked. Even if you wear the longest dress you own, you will still be pulling it down as if it were too short because God is pulling the cover off! Yet, as with the lancing of a boil, healing begins at the place of exposure.

You Will Not Exceed Your Leader

Whenever you come into the company of the prophets, you are going to prophesy. Saul should have known that when he came into the company of the prophets not to attempt to send messages in search of David.

Prophetic Principle #35

Come under the discipline of the Lord.

There is a spiritual principle here. Whatever the leader has, you will have. You will not rise above the leader. It doesn't matter how many dreams or visions you have, you will be in a prison there. God will never give more authority to the one who is under the leader.

When people in a church feel that they have exceeded their leader, they become frustrated, unfulfilled, discontent, and problem people within the church. We encourage people at our church who feel their needs are not being met to leave and go somewhere else. As long as they stay they will be discontent, and disturbed.

What usually happens after people have left to go to other churches is that they can't even find the niche they had at their former church. How many places will they go to? When they finally find a ministry that is moving with the heartbeat of God, they go there and want to give directions. When their feelings and ideas are not exalted above the pastor's, they feel as though they are not appreciated in that house.

It becomes a vicious cycle because they never learn to come under the discipline of the Lord. I have had pastors call me to inquire about those who have recently left my church and joined theirs. Later those same pastors would call to tell me they were having problems with them.

Prophetic Principle #36

We must minister out of relationship.

It's just a matter of time until the problem surfaces again. Usually problem people will have problems in the next work until it is dealt with. It's just a matter of time.

Relationships and Prophecy

> I Samuel 10:5: *"After that thou shalt come to the hill of God, where is the garrison of the Philistines: and it shall come to pass, when thou art come thither to the city, that thou shalt meet a company of prophets coming down from the high place with a psaltery, and a tabret, and a pipe, and a harp, before them; and they shall prophesy:"*

Here we begin to see a company of prophets. I believe those prophets were so interwoven that they ministered out of their relationship with one another. The Father wants to bring us to the place where we will begin to minister out of relationship.

When this occurs, there is a degree of light that doesn't flow in any other type of union. Life flows through the members of my natural body because they are connected and related to each other.

This is a day when God is connecting the "cousin" ministries, the "Marys" who will go by the wayside and the high places to seek out the "Elizabeths" who are pregnant with like revelation.

God is bringing people together who are pregnant with like revelation, ministering out of relationships.

"In House" And "Outhouse" Prophets

Even when the prophet Elijah died, Elisha, the one who remained, was so anointed that the widow who blessed Elijah was not left stranded. She was miraculously brought out of her of debt.

Prophetic Principle #37

A person in authority must first be a person under authority.

They ministered out of a relationship. I am no longer looking to minister in places just for the sake of ministering, but now I want to go into places to minister out of relationship. There is a degree of life that flows when there is relationship and people are coming together pregnant with the same revelation.

Submission and Prophetic Authority

"Then Samuel took a vial of oil, and poured it upon his head, and kissed him, and said, Is it not because the Lord hath anointed thee to be captain over his inheritance?

When thou art departed from me today, then thou shalt find two men by Rachel's sepulchre in the border of Benjamin at Zelzah; and they will say unto thee, The asses which thou wentest to seek are found: and, lo, thy father hath left the care of the asses, and sorroweth for you, saying, What shall I do for my son?

I Samuel 10:1-2

It is interesting that when God anointed Saul to be king, he was under authority. Notice that Saul was looking for his father's asses. If you are going to be a person in authority you must first be a person under authority. The measure of your submission will measure out the degree of your authority.

Prophetic Principle #38

Discern the difference between the cup and the will.

As Saul was sparing the king and the sheep from the commandment of the Lord that they be destroyed, we see that obedience is better than sacrifice. When Jesus went to the cross, we should not see the sacrifice, but that the obedience was better. It was the will of the Father. He said, "Lord, if it be Thy will, let this cup pass from Me, but nevertheless, not My will, but Thine be done".

There comes a time in life where the sacrifice might not be the will. We need to begin to discern the difference between the cup and the will. When we understand what the cup is, then we need to discern if it is the will.

People can make vows that are not right. A man in the Bible made a vow that he would sacrifice the first thing that walked out of his house unto the Lord. The first thing that walked out of his house was his daughter. God did not require that sacrifice from him, yet he was bound by his impetuousness to fulfill his vow.

We make sacrifices that are not the will of God. "I'm going to go on a 40 day fast." Well, that's nice, but is that God's will? God wants us to come to the place where we understand that obedience is better than sacrifice. The will should always supersede the cup.

There are many of you who are entangled in situations that God has never told you to get involved in. You are carrying the cup and you will never enter into His will. Some of you are in places out of sacrifice but not in the will.

Prophetic Principle #39

The prophet does not know and see all.

There is a difference between the cup and the will, but it becomes a different thing when the cup and the will are married. If it is the will of God for you to partake of the cup. Make sure that the cup is the cup of His will.

Prophecy and Imperfection

The prophet does not know and see all. God is the only One who holds that distinction. The Scripture says that we know in part and we prophesy in part. We can only speak that part which the Lord reveals unto us.

Many times God will hide things from the prophets. He did it with Samuel and Elijah. Not that they were out of God's will, but the Lord hid it from them. There are some things that the Lord leaves the prophet blinded to.

A prophet is not led by a prophetic anointing in his own personal life. He has to trust God and hear the voice of the Spirit the same way that you do. Sometimes people have a hard time discerning the difference between the prophet and the man, which is why I have to be careful about who I keep company with. They figure that just because I am a prophet, God reveals everything to me.

Prophetic Principle #40

Prophets are human, and they can make mistakes.

People can attach a mystique to the prophet to such a degree that they begin to look at the prophet as one who should never make a mistake, feeling as if whatever he says comes out of the mouth of God. They think that the prophet should be very spooky, spiritual and weird with a mystical voice and constantly spouting off "deep" revelations from "the other world."

Prophets are human, and they can make mistakes. Just as pastors, teachers and evangelists can all make mistakes, so can prophets. I have made lots of mistakes in my prophecies. The word was of God, and it was a perfect gift moving through an imperfect vessel.

Sometimes, you can look at a situation and discern God moving through it, even though it is not apparent in the natural. You might be hesitant in the Spirit because of conflicting external appearances. By not giving the word the Lord gave you, you have not given the word that individual needed to hear at that particular time because you looked at the outside.

You can give words prematurely, or deliver the word without wisdom (not apply wisdom to the delivery). Things that could be easily misconstrued and cause confusion should be said behind closed doors, not out in the open.

Sometimes you receive in part, and not understanding the part you receive, add other dimensions for clarity.

I remember a situation where an individual received a prophetic word about two of his children. This brother who gave him the word was praying one day, when the Lord brought this individual to his mind and told him to intercede for "a cookie and a candy". He didn't understand it.

He could have taken that to mean that God wanted this individual to go into a cookie and candy business. This was the only part that God showed him. When He went to this individual, he told him he didn't understand it, but that God had told him to intercede for cookie and candy and that he had been interceding for the last couple of days.

Prophetic Principle #41

God only gives you the part that you need to have.

"Cookie' and "Candy" were the nicknames of this individual's children. People can receive the proper impression in their spirit, but when they try to apply it, they go off. You have to give it to them as it is revealed to you, and let them deal with it.

God only gives you the part that you need to have. If He doesn't give any more, you shouldn't try to peep in and look for any more. I encourage people to ask questions when they are prophesying. If you get a check in your spirit, don't just bypass it and keep prophesying. Stop on your tracks and ask questions.

In New York, we would ask couples to come up. With one couple, I kept getting this red light, a caution. When I am prophesying and am getting that red light I know that I am about ready to step over into a delicate area.

As the red light flashed, I said, "Hold it, just a minute. Are you two married?" They said, "No, we live together." I stopped, gave them instructions on getting married, led them to the Lord, and then went back to giving them the word of the Lord.

Prophetic Principle #42

Stay away from interpretation and application.

If there is that check, you need to stop and ask questions. Never assume. Now don't do this with everybody, but there are times you will need to ask questions.

I know of one prophet who went to a place to minister to ministers. There were about 20-25 ministers present. They were apparently checking out his prophetic ministry, so they stuck a mechanic in there who wasn't a minister.

The prophet was going down the line, and when he got to the mechanic he said he didn't understand what it was, but that he was getting a picture of nuts and bolts. He said he must have a ministry that was going to be hard with nuts and bolts, but that God said that He was going to send him international.

54

That individual ended up having a relative overseas that brought a whole dealership or something into his hands where he went international as a mechanic with nuts and bolts.

Whenever something sounds as strange to you it will probably sound strange when it comes out, but just let it fall where it falls. If you try to figure it out you will miss it. Stay away from interpretation and application.

Prophetic Principle #43

Prophetic words must be judged.

Judging Prophecy

"Let the prophets speak two or three, and let the other judge".

I Corinthians 14:29

I believe that means to let the other prophets judge and discern the prophetic words which have been spoken. I Thessalonians 5:20 and 21 tells us to prove all things and hold fast to that which is good. The prophetic word that would come forth is perfect but it moves through imperfect prophetic vessels. This is why you have to learn how to discern that which is the word of the Lord.

There are times when the soul of the prophet intertwines with the word and God uses that, but you have to be able to distinguish that which is the soul of the prophet. When ministering from the soul, the prophet, even though he can be just as accurate, can be easily misunderstood.

When you are first starting out in the prophetic ministry, it is best to give the concentrated word and let the person water it down. Don't embellish it or elaborate on it. Speak only that which is given to you. This comes through discipline.

I grew up under a very strong leader. You didn't just jump up and start prophesying every time you felt a prophetic itch. You had to be sure it was God or he would embarrass you, and sit you down publicly before masses of people.

Prophetic Principle #44

Protocol is essential!

It was a form of discipline, you were to speak only what the Father would tell you to speak. Even if you were in the middle of a prophecy, he would interrupt you and tell you to sit down, because it wasn't of God. The man was an apostle of God, well established, and could distinguish the word of God from the soul of the prophet.

There are times when God uses the soulish person. We can see in the Scriptures that sometimes the prophets got very dramatic in their prophetic words. I believe that is reserved for those who are mature, who have an understanding of the ways of God.

It's one thing to have a gift or an endowment of the Lord, but it is another thing to understand the move of God or the administration of the Spirit. You have some individuals who while ministering, would have bad spiritual manners.

Some individuals have a tendency toward improper manners in the natural. One who is not disciplined or mannerly in the natural life, carries their independence and rudeness right over into their spiritual life.

The initial test that prophecy must pass is that it must bear witness. There should be something on the inside when the prophet speaks that should confirm or affirm that which the Spirit of God has already spoken in your spirit. It should bear witness to the truth. Any word that does not bear witness you should put on the shelf.

Prophetic Principle #45

Prophecy must be in harmony with Scripture.

The prophets are always under judgment. Any prophet whose word cannot be judged or weighed, needs to be watched. Some prophets who are very controlling in their delivery try to use manipulation. They can say something like, "Now, if you don't hear what I am saying, thus and so is going to happen to you." They bring an element of fear into it. They manipulate people with fear.

It is one thing to have the fear of the Lord, which is reverence, but it is another to begin to prophesy and use prophecy as a means of rule and domination.

Someone brought a very harsh word which did not have much seasoning. The peace of God was lacking in the delivery of that word. Another pastor told that pastor that he hoped he rebuked the spirit of witchcraft that was in there because the word was delivered purely from the soul with manipulation and control.

Sometimes God brings forth a very hard word, but you can tell it has God's grace and peace in it because He gives the individual the ability to receive that word. When God does surgery, He does it in a way that leaves you healed and whole.

Prophecy must be in harmony with Scripture. Any word that is not in harmony with the Scripture is not of the Lord. God will not speak contrary to His written Word.

II Peter 1:19 *"We have also a more sure word of prophecy..."*

(We need to understand that this Bible, this written Word, is a more sure Word of prophecy.)

> *"...whereunto ye do well that ye take heed, as unto a light that shineth in a dark place, until the day dawn, and the daystar arise in your hearts: knowing this first, that no prophecy of the Scripture is of any private interpretation. For the prophecy came not in old time by the will of man: but holy men of God spake as they were moved by the Holy Ghost."*

Measures

We have to understand the importance of measures, where things in the Spirit begin and end, so that in the delivery they will understand the measure we are to minister in. When God speaks utterances of exhortation, edification and comfort into the Body of Christ, He has a tendency to move the prophet beyond that into a measure of bringing direction.

Prophetic Principle #46

Understand the importance of measure.

Whenever there is a budding prophet who is beginning to move forward and to give directives, I don't encourage the body to move unless it is confirmed by the elders of the Body and until the ministry has been proven. Just as it was important to

"In House" And "Outhouse" Prophets

have a School of the Prophets in the Old Testament days, so it is important to have a School of the Prophets today and to instruct people in their delivery.

The nature of the prophetic ministry requires that it be established, confirmed and affirmed in a local church under strong insightful leadership. That is the necessary foundation to build a stable prophetic ministry. Anything else is sinking sand.

Chapter 5
Culture and Prophecy

If you analyze prophetic ministries very closely, you will discover that they have their genesis in the prophet's cultural experiences. I find it interesting that God used culture in raising up prophets in the Old Testament. God wants to take some of our cultural distinctiveness and use that part which is good as His unique expression and a manifestation of His presence.

Prophetic Principle #47

God used culture in raising up the Old Testament prophets.

Culture And Prophecy

There are no two prophets alike because each one has been reared in a different culture. I once heard an Englishman who, when he prophesied, was very articulate and proper. Somebody else, who may have been reared in urban America, could use proper "street" language to convey the same message. Another prophet might be from the Caribbean, and could deliver the same word with his culture's flavor.

Prophetic Principle #48

Your ethnic assignment is not an accident.

God uses our cultural perspective to bring the word of the Lord. Your ethnic assignment is not an accident, but it is part of your preparation for the call of God and the ministry that God has for you to fulfill.

Recently, I was reminiscing about how, when I was a little boy, I was sent to a suburban school. This was the first year busing started, and when I first became aware of racial issues. Before that, I never knew there was a problem. I remember my childhood impressions of being in the midst of riots and running for my life. I have asked God why He allowed me to be raised up in that type of environment. Now I am beginning to see a glimpse of it in my ministry. Now I understand why God would open up the door for me to go to the United Nations and to bring a word of the Lord addressing South Africa and apartheid.

Perhaps in the mind of God He was saying that as a little boy, He allowed me to be in a setting like that to prepare me for a day I knew not.

God places you and allows you to be impacted by certain cultures. I don't believe that you come from the place you come from by accident. I believe it is the birthing place, the beginning, the genesis of ministry to those God ultimately called you to touch and illuminate.

The School of Prophets included much of Israel's culture. Those prophets primarily dealt with the nation of Israel.

I discovered that oftentimes the word of the Lord may be correct, but cultural differences may prevent an individual from receiving the word from you.

Prophetic Principle #49

There is a difference between the gift and the man.

There are times I have been ministering where the people have received the gift and not the man. There is a difference. To some, the culture and upbringing of the prophet can be a blessing, but to others it can be offensive. You can bring a direct and forward prophet to a people who are more abstract and that prophet can be offensive to the people.

This is where the Holy Spirit uses our uniqueness to get a job done. We need to understand limitations and barriers. We must discern where we need to allow that expression to come forth and where it needs to remain silent because the grace is not upon us to minister to a particular people. We must understand prophecy and the purpose of race and culture.

Chapter 6
Progressive Revelation

God is always bringing us into progressive revelation. We go from one degree of glory to another. There was a glory that was with the children of Israel in the pillar of fire by night and the cloud by day. Then there was the glory in the mount of God when Moses went up to visit God that only Moses was able to dwell in.

Prophetic Principle #50

God is always bringing us into progressive revelation.

The children of Israel wanted to hear God along with Moses, but it was so awesome, so great, that they became fearful, and told Moses "Never mind, you just tell us what God says". In the New Testament, there was a glory that Paul says excelled the old. We go from one degree of glory to another.

I believe that the prophet's ministry continues to move on in a progressive dimension. It goes from one degree to another. The prophets began to prophesy in the Old Testament in types and shadows. Today we move in a different degree in that we begin to prophesy from the person of Christ.

Prophetic Principle #51

There is no end to the Body of Christ.

Jesus Christ is the Prophet who is speaking in the church. In Him, the fullness of the Godhead dwells bodily. We have heard prophetic words since the 40's. With the outpouring of revival in the 40's and 50's, there was a new glory and a higher dimension. They prophesied according to the revelation and illumination that they received and yet we can see that God is moving us onward to progressive truth.

We also understand that there is no end to the Body of Christ. There will be other aspects of God that will begin to be unveiled and that need to be spoken forth because there is no end to God.

One winter a pastor had met this man, who was really an angel because there were no footprints in the snow. He began to tell him of some things that were going to happen to him in his life, ministry, and church. He told him he would visit him one more time before he would take him out of this life.

Prophetic Principle #52

Words are seeds.

When the angel left the pastor, he thought to himself: When you think you have exhausted all the knowledge of God and have learned everything there is to learn about God, the Father begins to pull back the veil and show you a million years of knowledge that had not been tapped. There are things you are hearing today that you did not hear ten years ago.

"When a prophet speaketh in the name of the Lord, if the thing follow not, nor come to pass, that is the thing which the Lord hath not spoken, but the prophet hath spoken it presumptuously: thou shalt not be afraid of him."

Deuteronomy 18:22

When the prophet speaks, and it is the word of the Lord, that word has the power in itself to bring forth that which God has spoken.

Progressive Revelation

Words are seeds. Notice that you do not take a seed and teach a seed what to do. As long as the seed is in the proper environment and under the proper conditions, it will reproduce after its kind. The light that is in that seed will come forth. The proper conditions also must be met for the prophetic word that is spoken to come to fruition.

Old Testament prophets spoke so profoundly that it seemed as though everything they prophesied was in the here and now. When the word of the Lord comes forth the prophet may have to warn the recipient that it is something that will happen in the future. The nowness of God causes things to seem like they are right there in the present because it is in the Spirit.

Prophetic Principle #53

We must be open to change.

That's why the word says "Now faith is the substance of things hoped for, the evidence of things not seen." "Now" faith is.

You may have seen the seed of truth there but you did not see the full blossoming of the truth, the full maturation of that seed. We have not seen the fullness of the prophetic ministry.

The Holy Spirit is starting to show me some things that will become the norm in the Church. That which

He has done among us is a genesis of what you are going to see, it will become the norm in the Church.

When the Body comes together, the company of prophets will begin to speak and share. Each one will share in the meetings and we will see the full revelation of what God is doing.

For God to bring forth the fullness of the prophetic ministry in the church we must be open to change. We are going to go through a transformation, moving from one stage to another. When the anointing comes upon you it changes you into a vessel of God.

I Samuel 10:6 *"And the Spirit of the Lord will come upon thee, and thou shalt prophesy with them, and shalt be turned into another man."*

After Saul had come into the company of the prophets, he was turned into "another man" because God wanted to give him new thoughts, new emotions, and wanted to take total possession of him.

Prophetic Principle #54

The Lord wants to elevate your thinking.

Whenever you come into a new work, there is a transformation that takes place. Some people come in so beat up and beat down that God takes them and changes them so that they walk like kings. They are

69

given purpose and direction. Transformation takes place from the inside out. Oftentimes, the Lord wants to elevate your thinking.

I love to dream big. I don't just dream for the sake of dreaming, but rather, I plan to work them out. I cast off anything that is unprofitable.

In the parable of the talents, we see that when their Lord returned, every one of them had turned a profit, save one who gave back what he was given. The Lord called him a slothful, unprofitable servant. If after being in a place for three months, all you have is what you came with, they need to do away with you. The Scripture says that they cast them into outer darkness.

There are some people who never move out into the things of God, even though they continually receive the word. They are unprofitable and God does not tolerate them in the kingdom.

There are some folks who are so inflexible that they are satisfied with what they have and want to hold on to it. People want the church to make some changes, but they won't accommodate any additions to their life.

SO TRUE

Prophetic Principle #55

Be a person of purpose and destiny.

These people become unprofitable. Many churches have those who are still at the same place they were when they first came. Are they servants? Yes, but unprofitable. They don't move on to produce more. The Lord has told me we need to get rid of them and not spend so much time with them. Some I will carry around for a season, but when I don't see any advancement made, they will be cast out. They aren't good for anything. They are wasting God's time, my time, and your time. That time can be invested in someone else who would appreciate it and go forward. Some people never click into the vision of the ministry because they are not people of purpose or destiny, they just wander aimlessly. They are a liability to the ministry.

"Then went he also to Ramah, and came to a great well that is in Sechu: and he asked and said, Where are Samuel and David? And one said, Behold, they be at Naioth in Ramah.

And he went thither to Naioth in Ramah: and the Spirit of God was upon him also, and he went on, and prophesied, until he came to Naioth in Ramah.

And he stripped off his clothes also, and prophesied before Samuel in like manner, and lay down naked all that day and all that night. Wherefore they say, Is Saul also among the prophets?"

I Samuel 19:22-24

Progressive Revelation

In this passage, Saul had lost his kingly anointing and was hunting David (God's anointed) like a savage animal. He was no longer fulfilling his divine purpose. He had turned from an asset to the purposes of God to a liability. When the Scripture said that he laid down naked, it doesn't mean that he was nude. He pulled off his tunic, or his kingly manner.

When God strips a man of his ministry who has become part and parcel of it, the next best thing for that man to do is to lay down and die. The separation is like the departing of the spirit from the body.

When God took Aaron up into the mountain and told him to take off his priestly garment, which denoted ministry, that's when his day was over and he departed.

Prophetic Principle #56

The purpose of God is our sole reason for living.

We need to be so locked up into the purpose of God that it becomes our sole reason for living. Once our purpose ceases, our function in this life ceases.

This is when you understand what it means to be a man or a woman of destiny. When you understand destiny, you will begin to realize that for this cause you were born. It was once said that anything not worth dying for is not worth living for. You need to understand what purpose you were born for. Only for that purpose will you live.

You need to understand where you will spend the end of your days. I am not talking about laying out in the sun in Florida after retirement. We need to look into the purpose of God and know where He wants us to spend the end of our days. Do away with the luxurious, material things. Who are you to affect?

A missionary had gotten old on the mission field, and the board was suggesting that she go home, be with her family and die. She told them, "No. I told them how to live. Now I am going to teach them how to die." She understood her purpose in the place of destiny.

Prophetic Principle #57

Impartation then departation.

The Psalmist asks the Lord to teach us how to number our days. You need to understand the number of your days. When you understand the number of your days, you will understand the season of your departing. Before there can be departation, there must first be impartation. You will know those to whom you must impart to before you depart this life.

Chapter 7
Motives of the Heart

The word of the Lord that God may drop in one's spirit must be judged as to whether it is time to deliver it or if this is just something that God is revealing to the prophet. Will it bring forth a measure of life, or do I want to deliver this for effect? We need to check the motives of our heart for delivering because sometimes the word may be right, but the spirit in which we would deliver it in is wrong.

Prophetic Principle #58

The prophet ministers his spirit to the people.

Paul never talked about how a person handled the Scripture when he talked about the ministry of an elder. He said to be the husband of one wife, let their children be under subjection, be able to rule their own home well. When a man ministers, he is ministering his spirit unto the people. It is the character. When the prophet ministers to the people, it is his spirit that ministers to the people.

A word given in the wrong spirit cannot have the appropriate impact because it was not delivered by a moving of the Holy Spirit.

Prophetic Principle #59

Discern the motives that are in the gifts.

Motive of Gifts

II Kings 5 talks about the time when Naaman was told by the prophet to go dip in the Jordan.

> *"Then went he down, and dipped himself seven times in Jordan, according to the saying of the man of God: and his flesh came again like unto the flesh of a little child, and he was clean.*
>
> *And he returned to the man of God, he and all his company, and came, and stood before him: and he said, Behold, now I know that there is no God in all the earth, but in Israel: now therefore, I pray thee, take a blessing of thy servant.*

But he said, As the Lord liveth, before whom I stand, I will receive none. And he urged him to take it; but he refused."

II Kings 5:14-16

The prophet was about to get richly blessed because Naaman was very wealthy. It was up to the prophet whether he would receive it or not. I would like to believe that the prophet discerned the motive that was behind the gift. We have to learn how to discern the motives that are in the gifts.

The Spirit of God told me once that I was not to receive someone's gift. When I told them that, they wanted to know why. I told them that the spirit in which they were giving was cursing the treasury. They said they understood because they had been giving in the wrong spirit. Can you imagine that if countless men of God would have done that when they felt a check in their spirit, a lot of problems would have been alleviated?

Prophetic Principle #60

Don't sell your birthright.

You need to discern the motive that is behind the gift being given. When we were young in the ministry, there was a woman who wanted to mail us a gift, but said she could not mail it to our P.O. box.

Motives Of The Heart

She insisted that she had to have our home address to mail it to us personally. When I refused it, she got mad. We discerned the motive of the gift.

Many leaders have stopped pastoring and are bound because it is the gift that is giving the orders in the church. When we do that we become like Esau, selling our birthright.

A man in covenant understands how to discern the motive of the gift. The Spirit of the Lord told me once that there would be wealthy men coming to give me gifts. Some would be of the flesh and some would be of God. God told me to learn to discern that which is of Him because some would come with strings attached.

Prophetic Principle #61

★ There is always a Gehazi in the midst of the senior prophets.

The prophet discerned the motive in this passage. His servant, Gehazi, ended up heaping the judgement that was on Naaman upon himself, because he went to receive that which the prophet refused. Today, there is always a Gehazi in the midst of the senior prophets. They are trying to build their ministry and their reputation on the reputation of the leader because they can't wait for the release of the Lord to be bestowed upon them. They begin to step

out, but the motive of their heart is wrong. When
Gehazis are dealing with the areas of the prophetic,
you have to be very watchful.

I believe that there is a level of judgement in the
prophetic ministry which, if not dealt with properly,
can change that same ministry which was a blessing
to you into a curse. Perhaps Gehazi was a prophet in
training in the School of the Prophets. Because he
moved beyond his measure of authority, judgment
came upon him.

Your giving should be only a reflection of what is
in your heart. That's why people in debt, really have
spiritual problems. Their finances mirror the
condition of their soul. Once we begin to get our
covenant in order, it will begin to manifest in our
finances.

John said that he wished the people would prosper
even as their souls prospered. The prosperity of the
outer man is dependent upon the status of the inner
man. Whenever you get in debt, your finances are a
witness against you that something is not intact.

> *"And Elisha came to Damascus; and Benhadad
> the king of Syria was sick; and it was told him,
> saying, The man of God is come hither.*
> *And the king said unto Hazael, Take a present
> in thine hand, and go, meet the man of God, and
> inquire of the Lord by him, saying, Shall I recover
> of this disease?*

Motives Of The Heart

> *So Hazael went to meet him, and took a present with him, even of every good thing of Damascus, forty camels' burden, and came and stood before him, and said, Thy son Benhadad king of Syria hath sent me to thee, saying, Shall I recover of this disease?"*
>
> II Kings 8:7-9

Notice that it was all good things, and forty camels' burdens. The Lord has told me that if I treated the Lord's servants with the best that I will receive the best. You never saw the prophets in the Old Testament begging for bread. They were well taken care of.

Prophetic Principle #62

The prophets never begged for bread.

Muzzling the Ox

> *"For it is written in the law of Moses, Thou shalt not muzzle the mouth of the ox that treadeth out the corn. Doth God take care for oxen?*
>
> *Or saith he it altogether for our sakes? For our sakes, no doubt, this is written: that he that ploweth should plow in hope; and that he that thresheth in hope should be partaker of his hope.*
>
> *If we have sown unto you spiritual things, is it a great thing if we shall reap your carnal things?*

If others be partakers of this power over you, are not we rather? Nevertheless we have not used this power; but suffer all things, lest we should hinder the gospel of Christ.

I Corinthians 9:9-12

Paul was dealing with the church at Corinth. When the Jews would work the oxen in the fields they would put muzzles on the mouth of the oxen.

This is the same way some churches work their pastor. They would have them working but not partaking of anything. The oxen would get weak and weary and end up dying prematurely. They would have lived longer and been more productive if they had been allowed to partake of the field. Those sowing and working should not be muzzled, but they must be ministered to also.

Prophetic Principle #63

Don't muzzle your pastor!!

The Old Testament has some principles of how they ministered to and supported the prophet. I know it is God who provides, but I believe that God has set the pattern on how to administer that provision.

God will provide in spite of you, but I don't believe that is in the highest order. God has given you the means to be able to bless so that you can receive.

Motives Of The Heart

I Samuel 9:3 "And the asses of Kish Saul's father were lost. And Kish said to Saul his son, Take now one of the servants with thee, and arise, go seek the asses."

Prophetic Principle #64

✗ Never seek God's counsel empty-handed.

(There is a principle here in the way that God is going to bring forth those who have been getting away with rebellion. He is saying to go seek them and bring them back to the fold in the place where God wants them to be).

> *"And he passed through mount Ephraim, and passed through the land of Shalisha, but they found them not: then they passed through the land of Shalim, and there they were not: and he passed through the land of the Benjamites, but they found them not.*
>
> *And when they were come to the land of Zuph, Saul said to his servant that was with him, Come, and let us return; lest my father leave caring for the asses, and take thought for us.*
>
> *And he said unto him, Behold now there is in this city a man of God, and he is an honourable man; all that he saith cometh surely to pass: now*

let us go thither; peradventure he can shew us our
way that we should go.
Then said Saul to his servant, But behold, if we
go, what shall we bring the man? for the bread is
spent in our vessels and there is not a present to
bring to the man of God: what have we?"

I Samuel 9:4-7

Whenever anyone went to see the man of God, they never went empty-handed. When you go to see a doctor, or a lawyer, do you go empty-handed? Why is that when you go to the man of God you go empty-handed? I wouldn't go to a man of God empty-handed, just as when I go to a natural doctor I wouldn't go empty-handed. I definitely wouldn't go to the man or woman of God who will doctor my spiritual ills empty-handed!

Prophetic Principle #65

The prophet and recipient have prophetic responsibility.

Oftentimes, we will try to get the prophet off into the corner alone and we will have a thousand and one questions and we still haven't blessed him with one single dime. You are wearing him out.

Saul was concerned about what they could bring. Evidently it was a custom in Israel during that day that if you went to see the man of God, you made sure you had a gift in your hand.

> *And the servant answered Saul again, and said, Behold, I have here at hand the fourth part of a shekel of silver: that will I give to the man of God, to tell us our way.*
>
> *(Beforetime in Israel, when a man went to inquire of God, thus spake Come, and let us go to the seer: for he that is now called a Prophet was beforehand called a Seer.)*
>
> *Then said Saul to his servant, Well said; come, let us go. So they went unto the city where the man of God was.*
>
> I Samuel 9:8-10

I believe the Lord wants us to start to understand these principles. I believe we need to deal with the full scope of prophetic responsibility, both as prophet and recipient.

The Genesis of a New Prophetic Order

In II Kings 2 we see that Elisha became the head of the School of the Prophets. Elijah had been taken out by a whirlwind. Elijah had been sent to Bethel, meaning the House of God.

Prophetic Principle #66

 An old prophet can sense a new visitation of God.

Bethel seemed to have been one of the locations of the School of the Prophets. The prophet needs to dwell in the house. We have too many prophets that don't dwell in the house. There is an aroma in the house when the prophets dwell there.

Elisha had commitment and loyalty to Elijah.

And Elijah said unto Elisha, Tarry here, I pray thee; for the Lord hath sent me to Bethel. And Elisha said unto him, As the Lord liveth, and as thy soul liveth, I will not leave thee. So they went down to Bethel.

And the sons of the prophets that were at Bethel came forth to Elisha, and said unto him, Knowest thou that the Lord will take away thy master from thy head today? And he said, Yea, I know it; hold ye your peace.

II Kings 2:2-3

Prophetic Principle #67

Elisha asked for a double portion of Elijah's spirit.

The prophets knew that Elijah was about to depart. Let me speak a word of warning. There is a move of the Lord and a visitation that is coming in the land, to the inner cities of America. The worst thing that could happen is that an old prophet can sense when there is a changing in the move of the Holy Spirit. It doesn't mean that because they sense it, they are to be a part of it.

There was a young prophet that was used mightily of God to restore the altar. An old prophet told him that an angel had told him not to do it in a certain way. The young prophet looked unto the old prophet and ended up dying because he missed his direction from the Lord.

There is a visitation that is coming. God will begin to shut down people and will turn entire churches back to God. Some of those old prophets are going to try to find their way into the new move of God and try to redirect it so that they can control it. If the watchman and the porters are asleep on their posts they will be overtaken.

Prophetic Principle #69

God will cause resurrection in your life.

God is going to begin to snatch men off the scene, not because they have sinned but because they have fulfilled their course for the race. Others will be moved off because they will hinder that which He wants to do.

And the sons of the prophets that were at Jericho came to Elisha, and said unto him, Knowest thou that the Lord will take away thy master from thy head today?" And he answered, "Yea, I know it; hold ye your peace."

And Elijah said unto him, Tarry, I pray thee, here; for the Lord hath sent me to Jordan. And he said, As the Lord liveth, and as thy soul liveth, I will not leave thee. And they two went on.

And fifty men of the sons of the prophets went, and stood to view afar off: and they two stood by Jordan.

And Elijah took his mantle, and wrapped it together, and smote the waters, and they were divided hither and thither, so that they two went over on dry ground.

And it came to pass, when they were gone over, that Elijah said unto Elisha, Ask what I shall do for thee, before I be taken away from thee. And Elisha said, I pray thee, let a double portion of thy spirit be upon me.

And he said, Thou hast asked a hard thing: nevertheless, if thou see me when I am taken from thee, it shall be so unto thee; but if not, it shall not be so."

II Kings 2:5-10

Notice that Elisha didn't ask for a double portion of the Holy Spirit, but a double portion of Elijah's spirit. You can't receive a double portion of the Holy Spirit because the Holy Spirit is unmeasurable. How can you receive double of something you can't measure? Whatever the spiritual leader has, the people will have.

If you want to know what the leader is like, watch the people. You can tell how the people are by the way they give.

Receiving the Spirit of the Man

Elisha wanted the double portion. I found it interesting that when Elijah was taken, Elisha cried, "My father, my father." He saw Elijah as his father. You will never receive the spirit of the leader until you can see that leader as your father. That's a harsh statement, I know.

When I see the word "father", I see the area of discipline. I believe it isn't just by chance that in the school they were called the sons of the prophet. There is a principle there. A lot of people want to hang around the prophet to receive the prophetic or to move in that flow, but they refuse to become the son of the prophet. They refuse to submit to the corrective hand that will apply pressure and discipline that will effect maturity in their lives.

> "And when the sons of the prophets which were to view at Jericho saw him, they said, The spirit of Elijah doth rest on Elisha. And they came to meet him, and bowed themselves to the ground before him...

And he went up from thence unto Bethel: and as he was going up by the way, there came forth little children out of the city, and mocked him, and said unto him, Go up, thou bald head; go up, thou bald head.

And he turned back, and looked on them, and cursed them in the name of the Lord. And there came forth two she bears out of the wood, and tare forty and two children of them.

II Kings 2:15,23-24

I received a word in 1984 from a prophet who came to my home and told me the Lord said that there would be those who would come that would mock me and call me bald head, as they did Elisha.

When they are saying "bald head", they are not referring to the natural baldness of the head, but that the covering had left, and was taken away. Because of that, they were actually mocking the work of the Holy Spirit. They had bald heads for their master was taken away from them. They knew it was the season for the changing of the guard, but didn't realize that a double portion of that spirit was resident within Elisha because God was making up the new head of the school.

God will always have a way of confirming His authority and verifying that He sits in the midst. He did it with Aaron's rod when He caused it to bud and blossom. There are times I think we need to see more of that. When God got into that rod, there was resurrection life in it. Aaron couldn't make it bud.

It's the same way with spiritual authority. It doesn't matter how much you push and shove, if God didn't put the life on the inside of you and the unction isn't there, you won't have the anointing to minister. All you will have is an empty rod with no life.

God wants to move us from empty words to where our words are filled with His life. There was a power there that I believe we will see coming back into the church.

The prophetic ministry was used for pointing direction, and for confirmation. In the New Testament, they went to confirm and to strengthen the churches, bringing correction and building.

We will begin to see the prophet's ministry more and more. They are in the land, and God will begin to bring them out more and more. We need to begin to make provision and train them. This is not controlling the Holy Spirit, but giving them tools to work with.

We need to allow that breath of resurrection life into our lives today. There are many things that are going forth, but we need to make sure that we are moving in His life. Lord, teach us how to hold the things that You show us until the fullness of time.

VIDEO CASSETTES
BY BISHOP E. BERNARD JORDAN

RACIAL ETHICS OF THE KINGDOM

Confronts the intrinsic racism that has permeated Christian doctrine. A Thorough study of the "traditional" teachings of the Church unveils a deliberate strain of racism that fosters white supremacy and eradicates the image of God within the African-American. It was this same strain of religiosity that soothed the consciousness of many and justified the atrocities of slavery in America. This series delineates the patent effects of such doctrine and restores the dignity of all races under God that were created for His divine purpose. 4-Video series $80

FREEDOM: THE WAY OF LIBERATION

A clarification of God's true definition of freedom and the resulting implications of the facade of liberty that continues to enslave the African-American community. The continuous assault of malevolent imagery that society uses to deliberately cripple the function of an entire race of people and deface their cultural legacy actually recreates Jesus Christ, the anointed Deliver of men, into an effigy that is crucified afresh on a daily basis. True freedom will emerge as the traditions of men are dethroned and replaced by the uncompromising Word of God that will cut every insidious lie asunder. This series will offend many who have been blinded by the hypnotic lies that have lulled their purpose to sleep, and challenge others to look beyond the veil of mediocrity and prejudice and behold the beauty of God's original intention towards men. This four-tape series is an unforgettable encounter with past, present and future as it proclaims the manifest destiny of the African-American and the Kingdom of God. 4-Video series $80

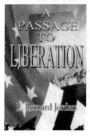

A PASSAGE TO LIBERATION

"A Passage to Liberation" is a thought-provoking edict against the dichotomy of society's offer of "Liberation" towards the African-American, versus their true liberty as ordained by God. The ingrained levels of prejudice that are encountered on a daily basis are indicated through the ethical teachings of the Word of God. Your spirit will be stirred to defy the implied boundaries of racial denigration, and thrust into the zenith of your capabilities through Jesus Christ. 4-Video series $80

PREPARATION FOR LEADERSHIP

A scathing indictment upon the insidious racism that permeates American society. Using Exodus Chapter 2 as his premise, Bishop Jordan delivers a powerful comparison between the pattern of oppressive leadership that requires divine intervention in the affairs of men and culminated in the appointment of Moses as the deliverer of Israel with the oppressive leadership that the African-American encounters within society and within the walls of the Church. Frightening in its accuracy, this teaching, though disturbing to the ear, is truly the Word of the Lord for this hour, for there are serious ramifications that the Church must contend with if she is to bring a solution to the crisis of woe in this nation.
4-Video series $80

THE SPIRIT OF THE OPPRESSOR

This series, The Spirit of the Oppressor, by Bishop E. Bernard Jordan, attacks the very fiber of societal influence that manipulates the gospel to justify racial supremacy. The insidious attitudes that permeate the Church are also addressed, for judgment begins in the House of God. By understanding that the Church is called to be the example for the world to follow, this series is powerful in its ability to expose the evil that lurks in the shadows of the "acceptable norm," and echoes a clarion call for deliverance from the lie that masquerades as the truth. Are you REALLY ready for the Word of the Lord?

4-Video series .... $80 also available as a book.

NO MORE HANDOUTS

In this series, Bishop E. Bernard Jordan addresses an inflammatory issue that has been instilled as a mindset within an entire nation of people. The American society has methodically caused generations of African-Americans to become dependent to a system that keeps them in a cycle of expectation that the government will always be their source of blessing. Bishop Jordan delineates the intention of God to bring prosperity to His people, thus charging them to turn their attention from the governmental system and discover the treasure that God has placed in their hands, for God is to be their source! This series is challenging and will force you to use your God-given abilities to thing creatively and generate wealth. You don't need anyone's permission to increase, for God has already decreed that you would multiply and wax exceedingly mighty!! This radical message is for a radical people!!

4-Video series $80

THE CROSSING

Bishop E. Bernard Jordan delivers a powerful teaching that defines the attitude that one must take as they begin to cross over their Jordan into the promised land. The paradigms of the old must be shattered as the image of change comes into view. One cannot embrace a new day loaded with old apparatus that is inoperative; old concepts that only brought you to a place of desperation and frustration. Rather, one must search the Word of God and renew your mind to Kingdom thinking that will bring elevation into your life. This series will sweep the cobwebs of mediocrity out of your life, and provoke you to a higher plane of right thinking that will thrust you into the path of dreams fulfilled. Straightforward in his approach, Bishop Jordan preaches a message that is inflammatory to the lies that have taken residence in your mind, and instills the purity of truth that is the nature of Almighty God. 4-Video series $80

UNDRESSING THE LIE

In this series, Bishop E. Bernard Jordan addresses a crucial issue in the Body of Christ -- RACISM. This series will captivate those who are true lovers of truth, for Jesus Christ is the Truth, and many have hidden Him and His cultural reality from the eyes of many. By conducting a thorough search of the Scriptures, Bishop Jordan identifies the Bible's description of Jesus that has been marred by the lies of those who wished to destroy an entire nation's concept of themselves, instead rendering theology that warped the image of God and denigrated them by teaching that they were cursed. Questions that have wandering in the minds of many for hundreds of years are answered as Bishop Jordan takes a strong stand to unmask the lies that have been masquerading as Truth. 4-Video series $80

LEGACY

In this series, Bishop E. Bernard Jordan expounds upon the African presence within the Scriptures. Combatting the misnomers that Africans were cursed by God and that they had very little to do with the unfolding of Biblical events, Bishop Jordan smashes the veil of delusion to cause the obvious truth to surface. During this season, God is causing a cultural renaissance to emerge. The oppressor of American society has lulled the minds of most people into a stupor of ignorance leaving them landless, powerless, and, once again, easy to enslave. The historical accounts within the Scriptures have been bequeathed as a legacy from our ancestors to proclaim the Word of the Lord against the sophisticated genocide that is affecting the African-American. A nation that ignores its past is doomed to repeat its failures in the future. Bishop Jordan brings clarity and balance to an inflammatory topic that is frequently misunderstood. 4-Video series $80

ECONOMICS: THE PATH TO EMPOWERMENT

This vital tape series by Bishop E. Bernard Jordan and Prophet Robert Brown deals with God's answers to the financial instability that has crippled the strength of the African-American nation. By defining the true motivation behind the onslaught of racism, Bishop Jordan and Prophet Brown give clear answers to the persistent societal obstacles that prevent most people from obtaining the true manifestation of God's intention for prosperity in their lives. The articulate questions that proceed from the heart of the nation shall be answered through the accumulation of wealth, for money shall answer all things. This teaching will expose the subtle racism that affects your financial future, and will provoke you into a mindset that will see obstacles as opportunities so that the full potential of God within you may express in your success!
2-Video series $40

NO LIBERATION WITHOUT VIOLENCE

This series will cause one to Scripturally discern the validity of the message of liberation that echoed through America during the 60's through Dr. Martin Luther King and Malcolm X. By holding their messages up to the scrutiny of the Word of God, one cannot help but conclude whose message was more palatable to society, versus the message that stood in the integrity of the Scripture. Challenging in its content, this series is designed to attack the shackles of passivity and charge you to recognize the brutal realities of today's society. You are called to understand the true liberty of the gospel that Jesus preached. 4-Video series $80

A NEW GENERATION

Bishop E. Bernard Jordan is at his best in this series which portrays the change in one's attitude that must take place in order to attain your maximum potential in God and proceed to your Canaan Land! Like Joshua, one must be ready to be strong and of a good courage as you confront racism in this day. This is a radical message to eradicate error and bring forth the truth! Cutting in its intensity, this series will show you how the Word of the Lord will render you untouchable when you are aware of your purpose!! Bishop Jordan defines the new breed of people that God is raising up that will know the art of war, understand and love their enemy as they embrace the arms of destiny fulfilled.
4-Video series $80

AUDIO CASSETTE SERIES
BY BISHOP E. BERNARD JORDAN

THE POWER OF INCREASE

This radical tape series by Bishop E. Bernard Jordan clarifies the principles of God that will bring increase into your life. For those who seem that they are in a continual financial rut, this series will place keys of deliverance that will thrust you into true prosperity.
4-Tape audio series $20

FROM BITTER TO BETTER

Everyone that has ever attained a measure of success has endured the gall of bitterness. There are many individuals whose current situations offend the very essence of their sense of righteousness. Yet God, in His sovereignty, will cause all things to work together for their good, since they are "the called of the Lord." Like Joseph, who endured rejection by his family, slavery, false accusation and imprisonment before he attained His purpose in God, so shall we tread upon the steps of adversity as we climb to the pinnacle of success. This series will thrust you into another dimension in God.
4-Tape audio series $20

KINGDOM FINANCES

How are Christians supposed to prosper as their soul prospers? What is the mindset of success? This series explores the power of money and the responsibility of the Christian to wield his power wisely as an example of good stewardship. These tapes are highly recommended for anyone who has had difficulty maintaining a Godly standard in money management 12-Tape audio series $55

THE FAMILY

The various pressures of corrupt societal influences have challenged the basic structure of the family. Bishop Jordan gives Scriptural premise for the line of authority that should exist in each family, and the development of healthy relationships. An extensive study, this series will revolutionize your home when diligently followed. 4-Tape audio series $20

PRAYER AND FASTING

The significance of prayer and fasting is discussed in this series. The many facets of prayer are discussed, as well as the mechanics of fasting and optimum results, both physically and spiritually. This series is a must for those who wish to develop their spiritual senses to a greater degree.
4-Tape audio series $20
ALSO AVAILABLE IN BOOK

THE HOLY SPIRIT

Is there such a thing as "The Baptism of the Holy Ghost?" "Am I still saved if I don't speak in tongues? What is the purpose of tongues? This series gives a detailed explanation of the identity and purpose of the Holy Spirit in the life of the believer.
2-Tape audio series $10
ALSO AVAILABLE IN BOOK

BOOKS
BY BISHOP E. BERNARD JORDAN

THE MAKING OF THE DREAM
Are you riding the waves to an unknown shore? Is God's will passing you by? Is your God-given vision a dream or a reality? If you aren't sure of your life's destination then you need to hear "The Making of the Dream!" These teachings are remarkable because they will assist you in establishing workable goals in pursuit of success. You God-given dream will no longer be incomprehensible, but it will be touchable, believable and conceivable! $10

THE SCIENCE OF PROPHECY
A clear, concise and detailed exposition on the prophetic ministry and addresses many misnomers and misunderstandings concerning the ministry of the New Testament prophet. If you have any questions concerning prophetic ministry, or would like to receive sound, scriptural teachings on this subject, this book is for you! $10

MENTORING: THE MISSING LINK
Deals with the necessity of proper nurturing in the things of God by divinely appointed and anointed individuals placed in the lives of potential leaders. God's structure of authority and protocol for the purpose of the maturation of effective leadership is thoroughly discussed and explained. This book is highly recommended for anyone who believes that God has called them to any type of ministry in the Body of Christ. $10

MEDITATION: THE KEY TO NEW HORIZONS IN GOD
Designed to help you unlock the inner dimensions of Scripture in your pursuit of the knowledge of God. Long considered exclusively in the domain of New Age and eastern religions, meditation is actually part of the heritage of Christians, and is to be an essential part of every believer's life. We have been given a mandate to meditate upon the Word of God in order to effect prosperity and wholeness in our lives. This book gives some foundational principles to stimulate our transformation into the express image of Jesus Christ. $10

PROPHETIC GENESIS

Explores the realms of the genesis of prophecy...the beginning of God communicating to mankind. The prophetic ministry is examined in a greater depth, and the impact of various areas such as culture and music upon prophecy are taught in-depth. The prophetic ministry must always operate under proper authority, and this factor is also delved into. This book is designed for the mature student who is ready to enter into new dimensions of the prophetic realm. $10

THE JOSHUA GENERATION

A book that rings with the sound of confrontation, as the Body of Christ is urged to awaken from passivity to embrace the responsibility to fulfill the mandate of God in this hour! The Joshua Generation is targeted for those who are ready to look beyond the confines of tradition to tackle the weight of change. Are you a pioneer at heart? Then you are a part of The Joshua Generation!! This book is for you!! $10

SPIRITUAL PROTOCOL

Addresses an excruciating need for order and discipline in the Body of Christ. By aggressively attacking the trend of independence and lawlessness that permeates the Church, the issue of governmental authority and accountability is thoroughly discussed. This manual clearly identifies the delineation of areas and levels of ministry, and brings a fresh understanding of authority and subsequent submission, and their implications for leadership within the House of the Lord. This is a comprehensive study that includes Bishop Jordan's earlier book, Mentoring, and is highly recommended for anyone desiring to understand and align himself with God's order for the New Testament Church. $10

PRAISE AND WORSHIP

An extensive manual designed to give Scriptural foundation to the ministry of the worshipping arts (musical, dramatic, artistic, literary, oratory, meditative and liturgical dance) in the House of the Lord. The arts are the outward mode of expression of an internal relationship with God, and are employed by God as an avenue through which He will speak and display His Word, and by man as a loving response to the touch of God upon his life. This book will compel the reader to deepen his relationship with his Creator, and explore new degrees of intimacy with our Lord and Saviour, Jesus Christ. $20

COMING SOON...
WRITTEN JUDGEMENTS VOLUME III

BREAKING SOUL TIES AND GENERATIONAL CURSES

The sins of the father will often attempt to visit this present genera-tion...however, those who understand their authority in Christ can refuse that visitation!! This series reveals the methods of identifying soul ties and curses that attempt to reduplicate themselves generation after generation. If you can point to a recurrent blight within your family lin-eage, such as premature death, familial diseases (alcoholism, diabetes, cancer, divorce, etc., then YOU NEED THIS SERIES!!!

Volume I .... 8-tape series..................$40.00
Volume II .... 8-tape series..................$40.00

WRITTEN JUDGMENTS VOLUME I

Chronicles the Word of the Lord concerning the nations of the world and the Body of Christ at large. Many subjects are addressed, such as the U.S. economy, the progress of the Church, the rise and fall of cer-tain nations, and Bishop Jordan prophecies over every state in America with the exception of Ohio. This is not written for sensationalism, but to challenge the Body of Christ to begin to pray concerning the changes that are to come. $10

WRITTEN JUDGMENTS VOLUME II

A continuation of the Word of the Lord expressed towards the Middle East, the Caribbean nations, America, and the Body of Christ at large. Addresses various issues confronting America, such as abortion, racism, economics and homelessness. A powerful reflection of the judgements of God, which come to effect redemption and reconciliation in the lives of mankind. $10

MINI BOOKS

1. The Purpose of Tongues $1.00
2. Above All Things Get Wisdom...................$1.00
3. Calling Forth The Men of Valor....................$1.00

ADDITIONAL VIDEO / AUDIO CASSETTES

This Time Next Year .... 2 videos - $40.00

Prophetic Connection .... 4 videos - $80.00

The Power of Money .... 8 videos - $160.0

Corporate Destiny .... 4 videos - $80.00

The Anointing .... 4 videos - $80.00

The Spirit of the Oppressor - expanded .... 4 videos - $80.00

Boaz & Ruth .... 4 videos - $80.00

How to Train Up A Child .... 4 videos - $80.00

The Power of Oneness .... 4 videos - $80.00

Laws and Principles of the Kingdom .... Vol. I & 2 - $80.00

Spiritual Protocol (Audio) .... 4 tapes - $40.00

Order Now by Credit Card
and receive 50%
off your total order

or

order by Check or Money order
and receive 40% off.

ORDER FORM

ZOE MINISTRIES

4702 FARRAGUT ROAD • BROOKLYN, NY 11203 • (718) 282-2014

TITLE	QTY	DONATION	TOTAL

Guarantee: You may return any defective item within 90 days for replacement. All offers are subject to change without notice. Please allow 4 weeks for delivery. No COD orders accepted. Make checks payable to ZOE MINISTRIES.

Subtotal	
Shipping	
Donation	
TOTAL	

Name: _____Phone _____

Address: _____

_____Zip _____

Payment by: Check or Money Order (Payable to Zoe Ministries)
Visa • MasterCard • American Express • Discover

Card No.: _____ Exp. Date)_____

Signature (Required) _____